GREEN BAY
PACKERS

PAT RYAN

CREATIVE C EDUCATION INC.

Published by Creative Education, Inc.
123 S. Broad Street, Mankato, Minnesota 56001

Designed by Rita Marshall

Cover illustration by Lance Hidy Associates

Photos by Allsport USA, Bettmann Archives, Campion
Photography, Duomo, Focus on Sports and Sportschrome

Library of Congress Cataloging-in-Publication Data

Ryan, Pat.
  Green Bay Packers/Pat Ryan.
  p.   cm.
  ISBN 0-88682-367-6
  1. Green Bay Packers (Football team)—History.   I. Title.
GV956.G7R93   1990
796.332′64′0977561—dc20   90-41256
                                                                 CIP

The French explorer Jean Nicolet, seeking a route from the Great Lakes to the Mississippi River, founded a settlement and fur-trading post in 1634. Almost 300 years later, that small frontier post would become a home for one of America's earliest professional football teams, the Green Bay Packers.

Green Bay, in northeastern Wisconsin, is situated on Lake Michigan, at the mouth of the Fox River in the beautiful North Woods—an unusual setting for a professional football team.

The Packers' home, Lambeau Field, is surrounded by

Don Hutson (#14) with Curly Lambeau and Irv Comb.

Starting at the top: The Packers posted a 10-1 record in their very first season.

natural beauty. Northern Wisconsin is a land of rushing rivers, pine forests and an abundance of wildlife. The people of the region have a love for the outdoors that is as great as their loyalty to their team.

The club they cheer for is one of the oldest franchises in professional football. They are a team with a rich and fascinating history. Their story began in 1919 with one man's dream; today that dream may become the magic of the nineties.

THE EARLY YEARS

Professional football began with some strange names for teams and players. It was a time for players like "Curly," "Bronko," and "the Antelope." Who played on teams labeled the "Fairies," the "Panhandlers" and the "Eskimos." In 1919, Curly Lambeau worked for a meat-packing company. When Lambeau asked his boss to sponsor a football team, the company responded by giving him $500 for equipment and uniforms. Lambeau became the team's manager, coach and star running back. He called the team the Packers in honor of the company that had helped get it started. The name stayed, and the Packers were born.

The players also had a strange look in the early days of professional football. They wore leather helmets without face guards and played "both ways." The roster of a team would be twelve or thirteen players, so a player was expected to play both offense and defense. Salaries were different, too; at the end of the first year, each player received $16.75. Regardless of the salary, the players worked hard for Lambeau.

An All-Pro in any era, linebacker Tim Harris

Three in a row:
Fullback Clarke
Hinkle led the
Packers in rushing
for the third straight
season.

Lambeau was a strict disciplinarian, and in his first year the team responded by winning ten straight games. The early Packers soon became a powerhouse in the new league and were champions in 1929, 1930, and 1931. The first dynasty in professional football had just begun. With stars like Cal Hubbard, Mike Michalske, Johnny Blood, and Clarke Hinkle, the Packers were taking their rugged style into the thirties.

Much of the Packers' success in the 1920's and 1930's can be attributed to Lambeau's innovative ways. Among other things he was the first coach to use the passing game effectively. But with this he had help. The Packers had the "Arkansas Antelope," Don Hutson, one of the greatest pass receivers of all time.

Don Hutson was slender and speedy, but he was also a very intelligent player. "One thing I did when I went with the pros," recalled Hutson, "was to modify my equipment. I had my shoulder pads cut down so they were pretty small and less restrictive. Also, I didn't wear hip pads. It gave me a little more speed, a little better maneuverability; it gave me a little edge."

Huston used this edge to become a star. In his eleven-year career with Green Bay, Hutson was named All-Pro nine times, and in the process he established virtually all the NFL pass-receiving records. Several of his benchmarks still stand today: most seasons leading the league in touchdown catches (nine), most seasons leading the league in pass receptions (eight), and the most consecutive seasons leading the league in pass catches (five).

Hutson was the terror of the league and the secret of the Packers' next three championships. The Packers always finished in the first division with Hutson. Despite any "stop-Hutson" defense, the Packers won championships in 1936, 1939, and 1944.

With the retirement of Hutson in 1945 and Lambeau in 1949, the first great Packer era came to a close. For the next ten years, Green Bay would endure hard times. Coaches Gene Ronzani, Lisie Blackborn, and Ray McLean tried their best, but nothing seemed to be able to shake the franchise loose. In 1958 the Packers experienced their worst season ever—one victory, ten losses, and one tie. It was time for a change.

1 9 4 5

What a game! Don Hutson caught four touchdown passes in a victory over Detroit.

THE COACH

Vince Lombardi was called "Coach" by most who knew him because they believed he was the ultimate leader. Lombardi established this reputation early. At St. Cecilias High School in New Jersey he not only won in football but took the basketball team to the state tournament and won. Lombardi had never played basketball, but he was able to use his skill as a motivator to bring out the best in the players. It was a characteristic that the Packers badly needed in their new head coach.

In Green Bay, Lombardi quickly established himself as a coach who wouldn't settle for anything but perfection. "You could have a bad day against just about anybody and hear about it," reflected Forrest Gregg. "The guy could be the greatest football player in the world. But if you didn't play well you heard from Vince."

Although Lombardi was a taskmaster, he also had a sense of humor. Max McGee, a star receiver for the

Fierce defense is a Packer tradition, (pages 10–11).

Star receiver Max McGee led the Packers with fifty-one receptions for 883 yards.

Packers, remembers: "I could make him laugh and I know he liked me because of it. He'd back himself into an emotional corner and I'd get him out of it. After we won a game 6-3 on two field goals he was furious. He told us to forget everything he'd taught us, to scrap it all, that we were going back to the basics and fundamentals. He reached down and picked up a football and he said, with a great sarcastic grin all over his face, 'This is a football.' And I said 'Slow it down a little coach. You're going too fast.'" The Packers were laughing and working their way to the top at the same time.

The top would eventually be reached with the help of a little-known quarterback from the southeast. Bart Starr, a seventeenth-round draft pick out of the University of Alabama, wasn't given much of a chance to make the team, much less lead the Packers. Halfway through Lombardi's first season, however, Starr got the call. From that day forward, Starr was Lombardi's quarterback, and he would go on to smash dozens of records: He completed a higher percentage of passes than any other passer in NFL history; he threw an NFL record 294 consecutive passes without an interception; he was the NFL's leading passer in 1962, 1964, and 1966; he was the Most Valuable Player in the Super Bowls in 1967 and 1968; he played in five Pro Bowls. Bart Starr simply became one of the best quarterbacks to ever play professional football.

But there were many heroes during the Lombardi era. The names read like the Who's Who of Football: Max McGee, Jim Taylor, Forrest Gregg, Paul Hornung, and Willie Wood. Even the offensive linemen became well-known; pulling guards Jerry Kramer and Fuzzy Thurston would thunder around the end, knocking down anything in their way. Kramer became one of football's most famous offensive linemen ever. His blocking played an important part in Green Bay's success and in one of the most famous plays in all of football. It occurred during the game that is now labeled "the Ice Bowl."

It was December 31, 1967, and the Dallas Cowboys were a long way from home. The temperature on Lambeau Field was thirteen degrees below zero, and the Cowboys were wearing gloves. Lombardi told the gloveless Packers, "You've got to be bigger than the weather to be a winner."

As the game progressed, the Packer defense knew that the cold was affecting the Cowboys. "One of the Dallas receivers let the cold get to him," recalls Starr. "It sure did tip off our defense. When Cowboy flanker Bob Hayes was going to be the intended receiver he lined up with his hands out of his pants. When he was not the intended receiver he lined up straight up, with his hands stuck down in his pants."

Eventually the Packers would find several flaws in the Cowboy armor. Late in the game, with the sun disappearing and the temperature plunging, the Packers were making their last drive. Starting from their own thirty-one-yard line, the Packers had driven the length of the field. After three short gains, the Pack was on the Cowboy one-yard line with only a few seconds remaining and the score Dallas 17, Packers 14.

Starr recalls the time-out huddle: "We had noticed earlier that Jethro Pugh, the Cowboys' tackle on the left side, charged too high on goal-line defense situations. So we knew a quarterback sneak would work. Jerry Kramer was confident he could block him. Rather than give the ball to the fullback we just sneaked it in."

1 9 6 7

Champions! Coach Vince Lombardi and his team celebrated their victory in Super Bowl I.

Quarterback Bart Starr continued his amazing career, passing for over 1600 yards and fifteen touchdowns.

When the pile was unstacked, Starr and Kramer had combined for six and the Packers had won the game 21-17. They were champions again, for the third time in a row and the fifth time in seven years. After the game Lombardi joked with the press: "We went for a touchdown instead of a field goal because I didn't want all those freezing people up in the stands to have to sit through a sudden death."

The Packers were the champions of the NFL. Until 1967 the NFL title was considered the highest honor in professional football, but after that the Super Bowl, a matchup between the NFL champion and the best team in the upstart American Football League, became the ultimate game. The Packers were the first NFL team to play the newcomers from the AFL. In Super Bowl I, the Packers showed the new league why they were the champions, beating the Kansas City Chiefs 35-10.

Super Bowl II would be Lombardi's last game as the coach of Green Bay. The Packers once again were victorious. They beat the big bad Oakland Raiders 33-14. Forrest Gregg and Jerry Kramer carried Lombardi from the field on their shoulders. "This," said Lombardi, "is the best way to leave a football field."

The following year Lombardi took over as general manager and appointed Phil Bengston as head coach. But Vince soon became impatient with this job. After a brief stint, Lombardi left Green Bay to become part owner and coach of the Washington Redskins. The Redskin fans quickly adopted him and looked forward to the future, but the man they called "Coach" became very ill. In 1970

Lombardi died of cancer. The entire nation mourned the loss of a truly great man, but nowhere was there more grief than in Green Bay.

Today, Lombardi and his Packers are legendary. Many believe the Packers of the sixties were the greatest team of all time. As proof of their greatness, there are now ten Packers from the Lombardi era in pro football's Hall of Fame in Canton, Ohio. They are Vince Lombardi, Jim Taylor, Forrest Gregg, Bart Starr, Ray Nitschke, Herb Adderley, Jim Ringo, Willie Davis, Paul Hornung and Willie Wood.

But as many would tell you, Vince Lombardi left his players with more than fame; he left them with his zest for life.

1 9 7 1

Rookie running back John Brockington led the Packers in rushing with over 1,100 yards.

THE LEAN YEARS

After the retirement of Lombardi, the Packers' fortunes began to decline. In fact, from 1968 to 1981 the Packers went through as many coaches as they did peaks and valleys with their seasons: Phil Bengston, Dan Devine, and finally, in 1975, Bart Starr.

Starr, like Lombardi, found a team with potential: John Brockington, the 1971 Rookie of the Year, was at running back, and Chester Marcol, Rookie of the Year in 1972, was a first-class-field-goal kicker. But unlike Lombardi, Starr was not able to develop the team into a consistent winner. Injuries to key players continually plagued Starr until 1981. The Packer fans, however, had been patient long enough, and they wanted excitement.

In an attempt to turn the team around, Starr traded for John Jefferson, an All-Pro receiver with the San Diego Chargers. As a rookie in the 1978 season, Jefferson led the

16

Like Starr, Hornung and cast, Sterling Sharp is one of the NFL's best, (page 17).

It was tough going for the Packers in the '70s, (pages 18–19).

For the first time since the days of Boyd Dowler (right), the Packers captured a playoff berth.

NFL in touchdown catches with thirteen. When he arrived in Green Bay, he teamed up with split end James Lofton to form one of football's most potent tandems. Starr also found someone who could get them the ball, quarterback Lynn Dickey.

The blossoming Dickey became the final piece in the Packers' offensive puzzle. The combination of renewed protection from the line, fine running by Eddie Lee Ivery, and outstanding receivers made the Packers an offensive powerhouse.

In 1982 Starr's team, with the legs of Ivery and the arm of Lynn Dickey, were finally in play-off territory. Green Bay posted a 5-3-1 mark in the strike-shortened season and grabbed a play-off berth for the first time in eleven years.

In the wild-card game, Dickey threw for 300 yards

against the St. Louis Cardinals. The Pack, in a 41-16 shellacking, gave the Green Bay fans something to celebrate. The Packers were two games away from the Super Bowl. The team to beat first was Tom Landry's Dallas Cowboys.

The game was another Dallas-Green Bay standoff, but this time the outcome wouldn't be the same as the Ice Bowl. Unfortunately for the Packers, this time the Cowboys had a quarterback by the name of Danny White. White fired for two touchdowns in the final quarter, and the Cowboys won 37-26.

The 1983 season found the Packer fans a heartbeat away from either victory or defeat. Five games were decided in overtime—an NFL record. Five other games were won or lost by four points or less. The Dr. Jeckyl and Mr. Hyde Packers were hard to figure out. Starr had to wait each week to see which team would show up. The fans' hopes would rise and fall until the end of the season.

The Chicago Bears stood between the Packers and the play-offs. In a race against the clock, the Pack lost out as a Bear field goal whistled through the uprights in the final second, giving Chicago a 23-21 win. Once again the Packers trudged home for the long winter, but this time without Bart Starr. He was relieved of his coaching duties on December 19, 1983. Starr's coaching record from 1975 to 1983 was a disappointing 53-77-3.

A week after Starr resigned, the Packers once again hired a favorite son, Forrest Gregg. Lombardi had called Gregg "the finest player I ever coached." The former All-Pro tackle knew what dedication meant. He had played a record 187 games as a Packer. The fans were hoping Gregg could instill some Packer pride in the new recruits.

Gregg knew that in order for Green Bay to return to its

1 9 8 4

First-year coach Forrest Gregg led the Packers to a respectable 8-8 record.

21

Packers' linebacker Brian Noble (#91).

former success the team would have to be turned upside down. In an attempt to do this, the new Packer coach tried to change the team's emphasis from offense to defense.

But despite adding several key players to the defensive line, the Packers' struggles continued. Over Gregg's four year term with Green Bay the club fought each year to reach .500. A return to past success this was not.

Disappointed in the results, Forrest Gregg left Green Bay after the 1987 season to become coach and athletic director at Southern Methodist University. The situation in "Titletown" seemed hopelessly buried in a winter sleep. Once again the fans were left waiting for a winner.

Linebacker Tim Harris was the team leader in sacks for the third straight season.

A NEW BEGINNING

Spring was just around the corner in 1988 when the Packers announced the name of their new head coach, Lindy Infante. Infante, with over twenty-five years in coaching, had been very successful as the offensive coordinator for the Cincinnati Bengals and the Cleveland Browns. It was hoped he could do the same in Green Bay.

The Florida native came to Green Bay and immediately won people over with his candor and wit. In just two short years, Infante made the changes necessary to bring the Pack into the nineties as strong contenders. "I feel good about where we're going," said Infante. "I feel good about the majority of people that are going to get us there."

Three players who may get them there are the three M's: Mandarich, Majik, and the Mouth.

The fans around the league are anxiously awaiting the development of the Packers' 1989 number one draft pick, Tony Mandarich. Mandarich, the most highly sought after

Clockwise: Sterling Sharpe, Brent Fullwood, Don Majkowski, Tony Mandarich.

lineman in NFL history, played at Michigan State. At 320 pounds Mandarich captured the attention of the national press when he threatened not to sign with the team but to fight heavyweight Mike Tyson instead. After the Packers had signed him, Infante joked, "Actually, for the amount of money we're paying him, we are hoping he can play the whole left side of the offensive line."

Mandarich is big enough to play the left side but he won't have to; he'll have plenty of help from another big man, Ken Ruettgers. "I think we're definitely going to have a solid offensive line, especially since we got Tony in the draft," said Ken Ruettgers confidently. Ruettgers, a six-foot five, 285 pounder with 5.2 speed in the forty, is intelligent as well. "He's a sharp kid," said coach Charlie Davis, "a student of the game who really works at it. He watches films and prepares on his own."

The Ruettgers-Mandarich combo may solve the pass-protection riddle, but Infante still wanted to hear from the defense. The voice of the defense would come from "the Mouth," Tim Harris.

Tim Harris is the kind of player that other teams hate, but the Packer fans love him. He is an impact player. Harris wants action, he wants turnovers, and he wants to hit people. After he hits them, he yells in their faces: "Gonna be a looong day. Woooohooo!!!"

"Hey Harris, you're a great player," Kurt Lowdermilk of the Vikings once yelled, "but you know what? You'll never make the Pro Bowl because you're such a loud mouth." Pro Bowlers are elected by the players but Harris doesn't care about popularity. He intimidates, taunts, and screams

1 9 8 9

He's Magic! Quarterback Don Majkowski led the Packers to a string of come-from-behind victories.

Tim Harris was named to the Pro Bowl, reminding many of former Packer great Ray Nitschke (right).

at his opponents. He's the Packers' designated cheer-leader. "Tim must lead the league in talking," says his teammate Kenny Stills.

But Harris's numbers show that he does more than just talk. Since his rookie year in 1986, he has been one of the league leaders in sacks. In 1988 he tied an NFL record for safeties in a season. Tim Harris couldn't be denied; in 1990 he was named to the Pro Bowl, mouth and all. Harris played the part of general on defense, and the other big M played it on offense—the one they call "Majik."

When Vince Lombardi came to Green Bay, he estab-lished his dynasty by securing Bart Starr as starting quar-terback. Lindy Infante ended any possible quarterback controversy by putting his stamp of approval on the young, exuberant Don Majkowski.

Offensive tackle Tony Mandarich.

Defensive leader Mark Murphy.

The Packer defensive line digs in.

1 9 9 0

Despite injuries wide receiver Sterling Sharpe continued to be Green Bay's leading receiver.

An athletic quarterback didn't impress Infante; he was looking for brains. "In the off season he told me something I'll never forget," says Majkowski. "He said, 'I want you to be a manipulator not a gunslinger.' So I became a student. I was in here every day, looking at film." Becoming the number one quarterback has not been an easy trick for Majik.

In 1988 the Packers, with Majik at the helm, set a club record for most passes in a season, 582. They also set a team mark for most completions in a season. Don was a threat as a scrambler as well; he was the Packers' second-leading rusher with 225 yards in forty-seven attempts.

Having gained confidence from this performance, Don Majkowski and the Packers were the team everyone was talking about in 1989. Week after week, Majik would come in and snatch victories away from the opponents. Majik possesses tremendous team leadership and a deep commitment to winning.

In 1989 Majik's daring runs and strong arm won several games in the closing seconds. His favorite receiver in those games was Sterling Sharpe. Sharpe, a number one pick out of South Carolina, can find the open field. As a rookie he caught more passes than any other player in the team's history. Together these two young players frustrated the defensive secondary.

Although the Packers just missed the play-offs in 1989, things may soon change. With another strong draft in 1990, people may quickly realize that for the first time in twenty years the expression "the Pack is back" is not just a worn-out phrase, but a rallying cry for the team of the nineties.